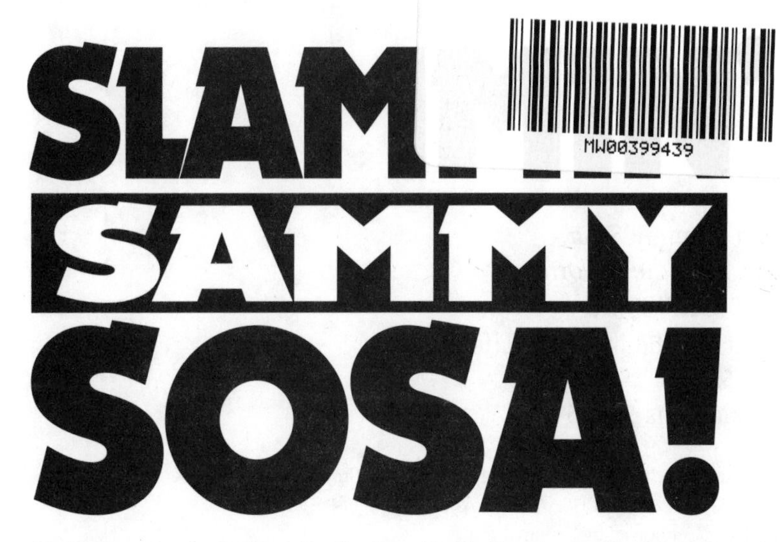

THE RACE FOR THE RECORD

Trade Life Books
Tulsa, Oklahoma

Slammin' Sammy Sosa:
The Chase for the Record!
ISBN 1-57757-065-0

P.O. Box 55325
Tulsa, Oklahoma 74155

Cover and text design/layout: Paragon Communications Group, Inc., Tulsa, OK

- To the incredible fans of America's favorite sport.
- To boys and girls everywhere—never give up on your dreams.
- To Lucrecia Sosa—for your faith in God and Sammy!

HERE COMES SAMMY!

When Babe Ruth hit 60 home runs in 1927, he dared anyone to break his record.

Thirty-four years later, in 1961, Roger Maris did just that.

Neither The Babe nor Maris were seriously challenged until 1997, when Mark McGwire hit 58 homers. But on September 8, 1998, after 37 years of waiting, before 43,688 screaming fans, McGwire set a new standard for home run hitters.

But it didn't take long for the next home run hero to match McGwire. Just 5 days after McGwire broke Maris' record, Sammy Sosa hit numbers 61 and 62 on September 13, 1998. Here's the story of Sammy's race to 62 and beyond!

#1—A MORE DISCIPLINED HITTER

Sammy Sosa began his chase for Maris—and his race with McGwire—with a homer to right field on the fifth game of the 1998 season.

Sosa has been known as a free-swinging hitter throughout his career, with almost three times more strikeouts than walks. In fact, he led the majors in strike outs in 1997.

But on April 4, 1998, the day he hit his first homer of the '98 campaign, Sammy signaled to pitcher Marc Valdes of Montreal—and the baseball world—that they would face a new, more disciplined hitter in 1998!

Valdes commented: "The only real mistake I made was throwing a pitch up and away to Sosa. Normally he tries to pull a ball like that. Today he went with the pitch."

SOSA BY THE NUMBERS

NAME:	Samuel Sosa
BIRTHDATE:	November 12, 1968
BIRTHPLACE:	San Pedro de Macoris, Dominican Republic
HOME:	Santo Domingo, Dominican Republic
FAMILY:	Married to wife Sonya, four children: Keysha, Keny Sammy Jr., and Michael
HEIGHT:	6'0"
WEIGHT:	190
DRAFTED:	Not drafted: signed with Texas farm system

POSITION:	Right Field
UNIFORM NUMBER:	21
BATS:	Right
THROWS:	Right
SEASONS PLAYED:	10
FORMER TEAMS:	Texas Rangers, Chicago White Sox
CURRENT TEAM:	Chicago Cubs, signed through 2001
ACQUIRED:	From the Chicago White Sox along with pitcher Ken Patterson for outfielder George Bell on March 30, 1992

Despite capturing two consecutive MVP awards in the American League, Roger Maris has never been elected to baseball's Hall of Fame.

SAMMY'S APRIL SHOWERS

Sosa hit six home runs in the first month of the season. Not bad. No one had yet guessed that his gentle April showers would turn into a torrential downpour in June!

AB	—	103	**RBI**	—	16
G	—	26	**BB**	—	11
H	—	35	**SLG**	—	.563
HR	—	6	**AVG**	—	.340

* THE ASTERISK

When Roger Maris began to make a run at Babe Ruth, he was scorned, first by the game's establishment and then by the fans. He hit his 35th homer on July 15—putting him 19 games ahead of Ruth's pace.

At that point, baseball's commissioner, Ford Frick, an old friend of Ruth, declared that for the record to be officially broken, it would have to happen in 154 games—the length of Ruth's season.

IN THE BIG LEAGUES!

Sosa made his Major League debut with the Texas Rangers on June 16, 1989. He went 2-for-4 with his first hit coming against Andy Hawkins of the New York Yankees.*

Sosa hit his first Major League home run on June 21, 1989, against Boston's Roger Clemens.

Sosa's batting average was only .238 on July 20, so he was optioned back to Oklahoma City (AAA). He was then traded to the Chicago White Sox on July 29.

The White Sox called Sosa back up to the Majors on August 22. In his first game against Minnesota, he batted 3-for-3 with a home run, 2 RBIs, and 2 runs scored.

* *Mark McGwire went 2-for-4 in his big league debut—also against the Yankees*

NOT EVERYONE WAS WATCHING!

When U.S. Senator Ted Kennedy introduced President Bill Clinton and Vice President Al Gore at a Boston political fund raiser, he proclaimed them as the "home run kings for working families".

When Mr. Kennedy compared them to baseball's real sluggers, however, he referred to the power hitters, "Mike McGwire" and "Sammy Soo-ser".

Which goes to prove, not everyone in America followed the Sosa-McGwire home run race. But almost everybody!

ON GOLF

***"I tried one time to golf,
and I hit everything foul ball.
I hit over trees, over houses."***

—Sammy Sosa

DID YOU KNOW?

A COZY LITTLE PARK

Charles Weeghman, owner of the Chicago Whales in the Federal League, built "Weeghman Field" in 1914. When he bought the Cubs in 1916, he moved their games to his new stadium.

When William Wrigley of chewing gum fame bought the Cubs in 1927, the ballpark's name was changed to Wrigley Field.

WRIGLEY FIELD

DID YOU KNOW?

When the winds off of Lake Michigan are blowing away from home plate, Wrigley is a nightmare to pitchers. The Cubs once topped the Philadelphia Phillies by a score of 23-22!

Wrigley, which officially holds only 38,143 fans, the lowest in the National League, is considered the most charming park in baseball.

Wrigley was the last Major League park to add lights. The first night game was played on August 9, 1988, forty years after the Detroit Tigers were the second-to-last club to install lights.

KISSES FROM THE HEART

After home runs, to the delight of fans everywhere, Sosa hops and skips from the batter's box, taps his heart with two fingers, and blows kisses toward heaven.

The gesture to the heart is for his fans, he says, and the kisses are first for his mother, and then for all his friends and relatives in the Dominican Republic.

Sosa leaps for joy as another home run leaves Wrigley Field.

HOME RUNS PER BAT

McGwire and Ruth dominate the greatest seasons ever, but Sosa made the list in 98!

PLAYER, TEAM	YEAR	AB	HR	RATE
Mark McGwire, Cards	1998	479	65*	7.50
Mark McGwire, A's	1995	317	39	8.13
Mark McGwire, A's	1996	423	52	8.13
Hank Aaron, Braves	1973	392	40	9.80
Babe Ruth, Yankees	1920	458	54	8.48
Babe Ruth, Yankees	1927	540	60	9.00
Babe Ruth, Yankees	1921	540	59	9.15

PLAYER, TEAM	YEAR	AB	HR	RATE
Mark McGwire, A's-Cards	1997	540	58	9.31
Mickey Mantle, Yankees	1961	514	54	9.52
Hank Greenberg, Tigers	1938	556	58	9.59
Sammy Sosa, Chicago Cubs	**1998**	**626**	**65***	**9.63**
Roger Maris, Yankees	1961	590	61	9.67
Hank Aaron, Braves	1973	392	40	9.80

**Through September 24, 1998*

SOSA'S 1997 SEASON HIGHLIGHTS

- Many consider Sosa to be underrated as a ballplayer. For example, he hit 40 homers in 1996, despite an injury that ended his season with 42 games yet to be played. Here's a few highlights from his 1997 "warm up":

- 36 homers—second highest of his career.

- Led the league with 174 strike outs.

- Hit his 1,000th career hit off Livan Hernandez of the Florida Marlins on August 20.

- Hit the 200th home run of his career on August 24 against Montreal's Steve Kline.
- Became the first Cub in 37 years to produce over 100 RBIs in three straight seasons—matching Ernie Banks' 1957-59 record.
- Sammy's 119 RBIs were his career best at the time.
- Started 161 games—the most by any outfielder in the National League.
- Hit the first "inside the park" homer of his career on May 26 in Pittsburgh's Three Rivers Stadium.

SOSA'S FAVORITE PHRASES

He can't match Yogi Berra, but Sosa is an entertaining interview! He is particularly interested in "telling the truth." Here's a few phrases that show up often in his interviews.

"I have to take my hat off and hand it to him."
"To tell you the truth."
"I'm not gonna lie to you."
"Believe me when I tell you."
"You don't wanna know, buddy."
"That's personal."
"God bless America."

THE "400-HOMER" CLUB

Now at 272* homers, Sosa could be only three or four years away from membership. Griffey, with 349* career homers, might make it in 1999.

McGwire began 1998 with 387 home runs, and crashed his way into Major League Baseball's elite "400 Club" with a four-bagger off the Met's Rick Reed on May 8.

Barry Bonds became the first man in history to hit 400 home runs and steal 400 bases in a career on August 23rd.

** Through September 24, 1998*

THE "400-HOMER" CLUB

	Player	HR
1.	Hank Aaron	755
2.	Babe Ruth	714
3.	Willie Mays	660
4.	Frank Robinson	586
5.	Harmon Killebrew	573
6.	Reggie Jackson	563
7.	Mike Schmidt	548
8.	Mickey Mantle	536
9.	Jimmie Foxx	534
10.	Willie McCovey	521
11.	Ted Williams	521
12.	Ernie Banks	512
13.	Eddie Mathews	512
14.	Mel Ott	511

THE "400-HOMER" CLUB

15. Eddie Murray 501
16. Lou Gehrig 493
17. Stan Musial 475
18. Willie Stargell 475
19. Dave Winfield 465
20. Carl Yastrzemski. 452
21. Mark McGwire 451*
22. Dave Kingman 442
23. Andre Dawson 438
24. Billy Williams 426
25. Darrell Evans 414
26. Duke Snider 407
27. Barry Bonds, Jr. 409

** Through September 24, 1998*

Sosa is also a threat on the base paths. As a member of the "30-30" Club, he has twice hit 30 home runs and stolen 30 bases in the same season.

A HOME FOR MOM

Sosa lived with his three brothers, two sisters, and mother in a tiny two-bedroom apartment on Calle Cincumbacion. Sammy slept on the floor.

After Sosa's first year in the Major Leagues, he built a home for his mom, Lucrecia, in San Pedro, which included the neighborhood's first TV.

After signing a big deal with the Cubs in 1994, he added a second story to his mom's house, plus added a satellite dish so she could catch all his games.

SOSA'S MAY POWERS

When it came to home run prowess last May, the baseball world was only talking about Mark McGwire and another pretty "fair" hitter named Ken Griffey Jr. But they didn't know what was coming in June . . .

AB	—	96	**RBI**	—	22
G	—	25	**BB**	—	16
H	—	33	**SLG**	—	.615
HR	—	7	**AVG**	—	.344

A BAD BREAK

Sosa first displayed his "record-breaking" power in 1996. After playing 124 games—he had played in every game so far that year—he was hit in the wrist by Mark Hutton of the Florida Marlins, and missed the rest of the season.

At that point in the season, he had already slammed 40 round trippers and 100 RBIs!

BASEBALL STATS

HOME RUNS MONTH-BY-MONTH

	MARCH	APRIL	MAY	JUNE	JULY
MARIS	—	1	11	15	13
RUTH	—	4	12	9	9
McGWIRE	1	10	16	10	8
GRIFFEY	1	10	8	14	8
SOSA	0	6	7	20	9

	AUG.	SEPT.	OCT.	TOTAL
MARIS	11	9	1	61
RUTH	9	17	—	60
McGWIRE	10	10	—	65*
GRIFFEY	6	8	—	53
SOSA	13	10	—	65*

**Through September 24, 1998*

RBIs

1.	Hank Aaron	2,297
2.	Babe Ruth	2,213
3.	Lou Gehrig	1,995
4.	Stan Musial	1,951
5.	Ty Cobb	1,937
6.	Jimmie Foxx	1,922
7.	Willie Mays	1,903
8.	Eddie Murray	1,899
9.	Cap Anson	1,879
10.	Mel Ott	1,860

AS BIG AS I CAN

"I swing as hard as I can, and I try to swing right through the ball. . . . The harder you grip the bat, the more you can swing it through the ball, and the farther the ball will go. I swing big, with everything I've got. I hit big or I miss big. I like to live as big as I can. . . . If I'd just tried for them dinky singles I could've batted around six hundred."

—Babe Ruth

BASEBALL STATS

THE "50 HOMER" CLUB

In 1998 Sosa joined 15 other men who have hit more than 50 home runs in a single season, and became only the fourth man to join the hallowed "60 Homer" club.

YEAR	PLAYER	TEAM	NUMBER
1998	Mark McGwire	Cardinals	65*
1998	**Sammy Sosa**	**Cubs**	**65***
1961	Roger Maris	Yankees	61
1927	Babe Ruth	Yankees	60
1921	Babe Ruth	Yankees	59
1932	Jimmy Foxx	A's	58
1938	Hank Greenberg	Tigers	58
1997	Mark McGwire	A's & Cards	58
1997	Ken Griffey Jr.	Mariners	56
1930	Hack Wilson	Cubs	56

**Through September 24, 1998*

YEAR	PLAYER	TEAM	NUMBER
1949	Ralph Kiner	Pirates	54
1961	Mickey Mantle	Yankees	54
1920	Babe Ruth	Yankees	54
1928	Babe Ruth	Yankees	54
1998	Ken Griffey Jr.	Mariners	55*
1977	George Foster	Reds	52
1956	Mickey Mantle	Yankees	52
1965	Willie Mays	Giants	52
1996	Mark McGwire	A's	52

**Through September 24, 1998*

YEAR	PLAYER	TEAM	NUMBER
1996	Mark McGwire	A's	52
1990	Cecil Fielder	Tigers	51
1947	Ralph Kiner	Pirates	51
1955	Willie Mays	Giants	51
1947	Johnny Mize	Giants	51
1996	Brady Anderson	Baltimore	50
1995	Albert Belle	Indians	50
1938	Jimmy Foxx	Red Sox	50

**Through September 24, 1998*

TO THE MAJORS

At the age of twenty years, seven months, Sosa became the youngest Dominican to make it to the Major Leagues.

The promotion came on June 16, 1989, after he hit .297, with seven homers, 31 runs batted in, and 16 steals in just 66 games with the Tulsa Drillers (AA).

In his first Major League game he went 2-for-4 with the Texas Rangers against the New York Yankees.

A "DOUBLE FIGURE" ROOKIE

Sosa played his first full major league season in 1990, hitting .233 with 15 home runs, 10 triples, 25 doubles, 70 RBIs, and 32 stolen bases.

He was the only player in the American League to achieve double figures for homers, triples, doubles, runs batted in, and stolen bases.

DID YOU KNOW?

THE GREAT ROBERTO

The great role model for Sosa and most Latin ball players is Hall of Famer, Roberto Clemente, born in Puerto Rico.

Clemente was a Hank Aaron-style ball player who did everything well both defensively and offensively. In addition to having one of the greatest "arms" in baseball history, he averaged .317 for his career, with 3,000 hits, 240 homers, and 1,305 RBIs during his 18 years with the Pittsburgh Pirates.

DID YOU KNOW?

On December 31, 1972, a plane carrying Clemente to Nicaragua on a mission of mercy for earthquake victims, crashed into the Atlantic Ocean. He was tragically killed—but not forgotten—at the age of 38. Major League Baseball named its citizenship award after Clemente.

Sosa wears number 21 in honor of his hero.

Roberto Clemente had a .317 career average in 18 seasons with the Pirates. He died on December 31, 1972, when his plane crashed in the Atlantic Ocean while enroute to assist earthquake victims in Nicaragua.

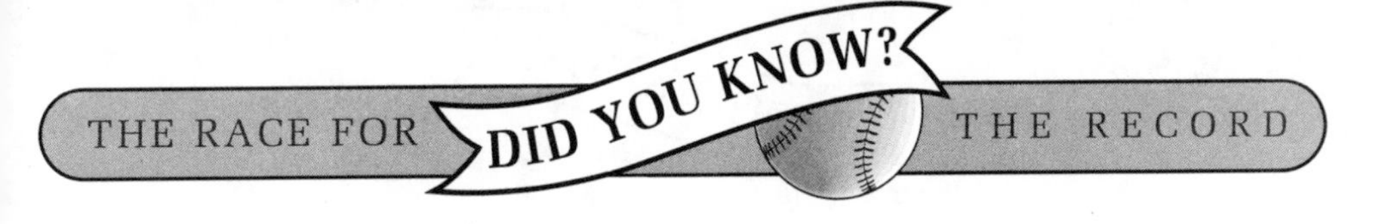

"THE COOLEST DAY OF MY LIFE"

Steve Ryan, a sports memorabilia collector, paid $10,000 for Sosa's home run ball number 61. He anticipated reselling it for at least $50,000, but instead handed it back to Sosa in exchange for a jersey, a bat, and autographed balls for his sons, Eric and Matthew.

After meeting Sosa, nine-year-old Eric declared, "It was awesome. This is the coolest day of my life."

MARIS HIGHLIGHTS

- Was recruited by the University of Oklahoma as a running back. When no one from the university met him at the train station, he returned to North Dakota.
- Made his debut for the Cleveland Indians on April 16, 1957.
- Traded to the Kansas City Athletics in 1958, and then on to the Yankees for the 1960 season.

DID YOU KNOW?

- Was American League MVP in 1960 with 39 home runs and a league-leading 112 RBIs. He barely nips Mickey Mantle for the award with 225-222 votes.
- Repeats as American League MVP in 1961, leading the league with 61 homers and 142 RBIs. Despite breaking Ruth's record, he again barely edges Mantle for the award, this time 202-198 in votes.
- Traded to the St. Louis Cardinals in 1967, where he played his final two seasons, appearing in two more World Series.

A MONTH OF RECORDS

Sosa set a Major League record for homers in a calendar month with 20, in June 1998, and also broke a few other records along the way!

- Sosa's record broke the Major League record set by Rudy York in August of 1937. The previous National League mark was 17, hit by Willie Mays in August, 1965.
- Sosa hit 21 home runs over a thirty day period, from May 25-June 23, which broke the record of 20 held by Ralph Kiner (August 14-September 12, 1947) and Roger Maris (May 24-June 22, 1961).
- Sosa tied the Cubs' record for home runs in consecutive games with 5, shared by Hack Wilson (1928), and Ryne Sandberg (1989).

DID YOU KNOW?

- Sosa hit 8 homers the week of June 14-June 20, tying the record held by Ralph Kiner (1947), Ted Kluszewski (1956), and Nate Colbert (1972) for home runs hit in one calendar week.
- Sosa set a new Cubs' record for RBIs in the month of June with 40, overtaking Hack Wilson, who hit 29 in 1930. The only higher output in any given month by a Cubs player was achieved by Wilson when he hit 53 RBIs in August, 1930.
- Sosa hit 10 home runs faster than any other Cub—twice! He hit 10 homers in 9 games, first from May 25-June 7, and then again from June 13-June 21. No other Cub player had ever hit 10 home runs in less than 13 games.

SOSA'S SCORCHING JUNE

The winds weren't just blowing in Wrigley Field—they were fanning the flames of Sosa's sizzling home run streak everywhere he played!

AB	—	114	**RBI**	—	48
G	—	27	**BB**	—	6
H	—	34	**SLG**	—	.842
HR	—	20	**AVG**	—	.298

BATTING AVERAGE

1.	Ty Cobb	.366
2.	Rogers Hornsby	.358
3.	Joe Jackson	.356
4.	Ed Delahanty	.346
5.	Tris Speaker	.345
6.	Ted Williams	.344
7.	Billy Hamilton	.344
8.	Dan Brouthers	.342
9.	Babe Ruth	.342
10.	Harry Heilmann	.342

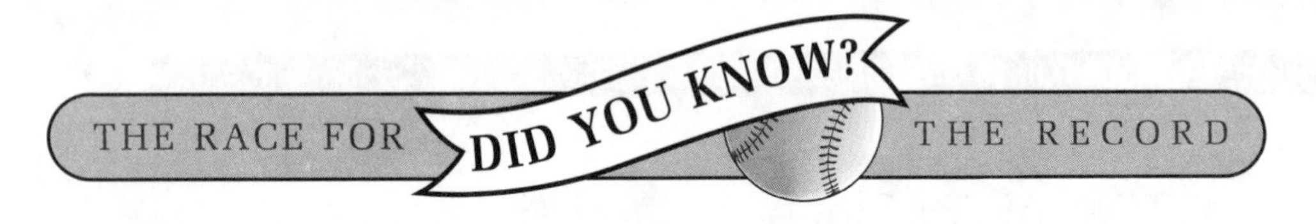

A YANKEE TRADITION

Before McGwire hit home run number 62 on September 8, 1998, and Sosa followed on September 13, a player for the Yankees had held the season home run mark for 78 years.

Babe Ruth brought the record to New York in 1920.

AN AVERAGE PLAYER

***"I never wanted all this hoopla.
All I wanted is to be a good ball player,
hit 25 or 30 homers, drive in around 100 runs,
hit .280 and help my club win pennants.
I just wanted to be one of the guys,
an average player having a good season."***

—Roger Maris

Trivial Pursuits

Intentional Walks to Maris in 1961?..0

Sosa career grand slams before 1998? 0

Sosa grand slams in 1998? 3

McGwire grand slams in 1998? 2

60 home run seasons prior to 1998?..2

60 home run hitters in 1998?..2

500 foot home runs by McGwire in 1998? 5

500 foot home runs by Sosa in 1998?..1

Games in which McGwire hit more
than one home run in 1998?...7

Games in which Sosa hit more than
one home run in 1998? 11

Days on which McGwire and Sosa
both homered in 1998?...19

**Through September 24, 1998*

HAMMERIN' HANK

The all-time home run king is Hank Aaron with 755 career round-trippers in 23 seasons. But Aaron never did make it to the "50 Homer" club. His best single-season output was 47 homers in 1971. He hit 44 homers three times in 1957, 1963, and 1966. Hammerin' Hank was the model of consistency, however, hitting more than 20 home runs in 20 straight years.

Hammerin' Hank Aaron was a model of consistency, hitting at least 20 home runs in 20 straight seasons. Here he breaks Ruth's career record with homer number 715.

CUBS "40 HOMER" CLUB

In 1996, Sammy Sosa became only the eighth player in Cubs' history to hit 40 or more home runs in a season. Then, in 1998, he surpassed them all, breaking Hack Wilson's team record that had stood for 68 years.

PLAYER	NUMBER	YEAR
Sammy Sosa	65*	1998
Hack Wilson	56	1930
Andre Dawson	49	1987
Dave Kingman	48	1979
Ernie Banks	47	1958
Ernie Banks	45	1959
Ernie Banks	44	1955
Ernie Banks	43	1957
Hank Sauer	41	1954
Billy Williams	42	1970
Ernie Banks	41	1960
Ryne Sandberg	40	1990
Sammy Sosa	40	1996

**Through September 24, 1998*

#41—A CAREER BEST

Sosa clubbed his 41st home run of the 1998 season—a personal best—on July 28 against Arizona Diamond Back pitcher Bob Wolcott.

He previously topped out at 40 home runs in 1996, the year he missed the final 42 games of the season because of a broken wrist.

WHO WAS THE YOUNGEST PLAYER IN MAJOR LEAGUE BASEBALL TO HIT A HOME RUN?

Tommy "Buckshot" Brown of the Brooklyn Dodgers was seventeen years old when he hit a homer off pitcher Preacher Roe of the Pittsburgh Pirates, on August 20, 1945. Brown played seven more seasons in the major leagues, hitting 31 career home runs.

DID YOU KNOW?

THE IRON HORSE

In 1927, the year that Babe Ruth hit 60 home runs, the man batting behind him in the Yankees' lineup didn't have a bad year either. That year, Lou Gehrig hit .373, with 47 home runs and 175 RBIs. His RBI record of 184 in 1931 remains the second highest total in major league history.

POWERQUOTES

AMERICAN PRIDE

"People in America have been so great to me. They appreciate everything we do in the field, and outside the field. It is unbelievable. Without America, I don't know where I would be today. I will never forget what America has been to me. Baseball been very, very good to me."

—Sammy Sosa

DOMINICAN BASEBALL

Baseball is a passion in the Caribbean, especially in the Dominican Republic.

There are five professional baseball teams in the Caribbean nation, each playing a sixty game schedule. At the end of the season, two teams advance to the Caribbean Series to face the champions of Mexico, Venezuela, and Puerto Rico.

DOMINICANS IN THE MAJORS

First Player: .Ozzie Virgil

Best Career Batting Average: . . . . .Matty Alou, .307

Most Career Wins: . . . . .Juan Marichal, 243

Most 20-Win Seasons: . . . . .Juan Marichal, 6

MVP: . . . . .George Bell, 1987, American League

Rookie of the Year: . . . . .Alfredo Griffin, 1979, American League

Raul Mondesi, 1994, National League

DOMINICANS IN THE MAJORS

Batting Champions:	Matty Alou, .342, 1966, National League
	Rico Carty, .366, 1970, National League
	Julio Franco, .341, 1991, American League
Most RBIs:	Sammy Sosa, 156*, 1998
	George Bell, 134, 1987
Most Stolen Bases:	Frank Taveras, 70, 1977
Best ERA:	Juan Marichal, 2.10, 1969, National League
	Alejandro Pena, 2.48, 1984, National League

** Through September 24, 1998*

DOMINICANS IN THE MAJORS

First Hall of Famer: . . . . .Juan Marichal

First Manager: . . . . .Felipe Alou, Montreal Expos, 1994-present

Manager of the Year: . . . . . . .Felipe Alou, National League, 1994

Career Pinch Hits: . . . . .Manny Mota, 150—Most in Major League history

Most Brothers: . . . . .Jesus, Matty, and Felipe Alou

Gold Gloves: . . . . .Cesar Cedeno, Houston Astros, 5
Cesar Geronimo, Cincinnati Reds, 3

CUBS HOME RUN HEROES

1. Ernie Banks 512
2. Billy Williams 392
3. Ron Santo. 337
4. Ryne Sandberg 282
5. **Sammy Sosa. 272***
6. Gabby Hartnett 231
7. Bill Nicholson 205
8. Hank Sauer. 198
9. Hack Wilson. 190
10. Andre Dawson 174

** Through September 24, 1998*

CHILD PRODIGY

Sosa was too busy helping support his family to begin playing organized baseball until he was 14 years old, an age at which many players have already honed their skills.

The Philadelphia Phillies took notice of his natural abilities and signed him to a deal at age 15, but baseball officials nullified the contract because of his age.

Sosa signed his first professional contract on July 30, 1985, at the age of 16, with scout Omar Minaya of the Texas Rangers. Sosa's signing bonus was $3,500.

SOSA'S 1998 CUBS' RECORDS

- Homers in a season: 65*
- Multiple home run games: 11
- Season homers at Wrigley Field: 35*
- Season homers on the road: 30*
- Sosa is still chasing Hack Wilson's record of 423 total bases, set in 1930. Sosa has 398.

** Through September 24, 1998*

Like his hero, Roberto Clemente, Sosa is a complete baseball player, who has great speed and a dangerous arm in the outfield.

Unbreakable Records?

Records are made to be broken, but here are a few that probably won't be challenged any time soon:

Season Batting Average: .426	Nap Lajoie (1901) 97 years.
Career Batting Average: .366	Ty Cobb (1928) 70 years.
Consecutive Games with a Hit: 56	Joe DiMaggio (1941) 57 years.
Consecutive Games Played: 2,632	Cal Ripken Jr. (1998).

Unbreakable Records?

Pitching Victories in a Season: 41	Jack Chesbro (1904) 94 years.
Career Home Runs: 755	Hank Aaron (1976) 22 years.
RBIs in a Season: 190	Hack Wilson (1930) 68 years.
Career hits: 4,256	Pete Rose (1986) 12 years.
Strikeouts in a season: 383	Nolan Ryan (1973) 25 years.
Team victories in a season: 116	Chicago Cubs (1906) 92 years.

THE PATH TO GLORY

Sosa, born in San Pedro de Macoris, a baseball-crazy town in the Dominican Republic, grew up selling oranges and shining shoes to help support his widowed mother, four brothers, and two sisters.

He received the equivalent of 10 cents per orange and 25 cents per shine for his labors. Now he makes more than $16 million per year.

Hits

1.	Pete Rose	4256	6.	Carl Yastrzemski	3419
2.	Ty Cobb	4189	7.	Honus Wagner	3415
3.	Hank Aaron	3771	8.	Eddie Collins	3315
4.	Stan Musial	3630	9.	Willie Mays	3283
5.	Tris Speaker	3514	10.	Nap Lajoie	3242

A LOYAL NATIVE SON

At home in the Dominican Republic, Slammin' Sammy Sosa is loved for more than his ability to belt homers over the outfield fence. His purchase of 250 computers to help Dominican children receive a proper education won him the affection of many, especially in his hometown of San Pedro de Macoris. And when the local fire department needed an ambulance, he pitched in for that too.

DID YOU KNOW?

Closest to his heart has been the establishment of a baseball academy in his hometown, where talented Dominican players receive free room and board, uniforms, and equipment. Such an endeavor provides promising young people (many of whom are locked in the grip of poverty) with the necessities of life while they work toward realizing their dreams. It's Sammy's way of ensuring that there will continue to be native sons like himself whose accomplishments provide a sense of pride for those back home.

POWERQUOTES

A HACKER?

"Sammy used to be just a hacker and a slasher. But he's realized he doesn't have to hit the first pitch out of the ballpark. What's wrong with hitting the fourth pitch out of the ballpark?"

—Billy Williams

(Cubs' coach and Hall of Famer.)

A BAD CENTURY?

T-shirts in Chicago read, "Any Team Can Have A Bad Century," in reference to their beloved Cubs.

The Cubs haven't been to the World Series since 1945, and last won it in 1908.

But who knows what can happen when a 29-year-old from the Dominican Republic puts a team on his shoulders and starts hitting homers?!

SOSA'S CAREER BESTS

- 6 hits in one game, on July 2, 1993, against Colorado.
- 9 consecutive hits from June 30-July 2, 1993.
- 6 RBIs in a single game on September 13, 1998—the day he hit home run number 63.
- 4 stolen bases in one game, against Los Angeles on September 29, 1993.
- 4 10-game hitting streaks.

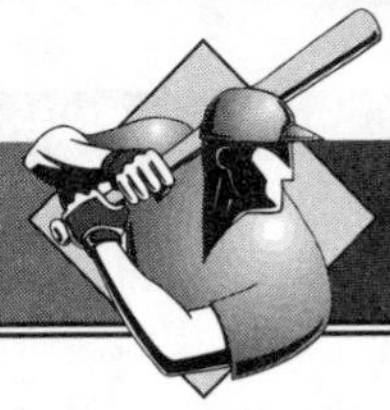

THE RACE TO 62

In 1927, Ruth and Gehrig battled for the home run crown mark of the season, but Babe pulled away from Lou with a final count of 60 to 54.

In 1961, Maris and Mantle battled almost the entire season, but Mantle ended up with an infected hip after a flu shot, and Maris won the race 61-54.

But the greatest home run race year ever is now, in 1998. Four men have a strong shot at hitting more than 50 homers. Ken Griffey Jr. and Greg Vaughn had remarkable years, but the real race was McGwire vs. Sosa for the final tally! Follow their road to the record and beyond as compared to Roger Maris' 1961 record-setting season.

BASEBALL STATS

NO.	MARIS	McGWIRE	SOSA
1	April 26 vs. Detroit Paul Foytack	March 31 vs. Los Angeles Ramon Martinez	April 4 vs. Montreal Marc Valdes
2	May 3 vs. Minnesota Pedro Ramos	April 2 vs. Los Angeles Frank Lankford	April 11 vs. Montreal Anthony Telford
3	May 6 vs. Los Angeles Eli Grba	April 3 vs. San Diego Mark Langston	April 15 vs. N.Y. Mets Dennis Cook
4	May 17 vs. Washington Pete Burnside	April 4 vs. San Diego Don Wengert	April 23 vs. San Diego Dan Miceli
5	May 19 vs. Cleveland Jim Perry	April 14 vs. Arizona Jeff Suppan	April 24 vs. Los Angeles Ismael Valdes
6	May 20 vs. Cleveland Gary Bell	April 14 vs. Arizona Jeff Suppan	April 27 vs. San Diego Joey Hamilton
7	May 21 vs. Baltimore Chuck Estrade	April 14 vs. Arizona Barry Manuel	May 3 vs. St. Louis Cliff Politte
8	May 23 vs. Boston Gene Conley	April 17 vs. Philadelphia Matt Whiteside	May 16 vs. Cincinnati Scott Sullivan
9	May 28 vs. Chicago White Sox Cal McLish	April 21 vs. Montreal Trey Moore	May 22 vs. Atlanta Greg Maddux

NO.	MARIS	McGWIRE	SOSA
10	May 30 vs. Boston Gene Conley	April 25 vs. Philadelphia Jerry Spradlin	May 25 vs. Atlanta Kevin Millwood
11	May 30 vs. Boston Mike Fornieles	April 30 vs. Chicago Cubs Marc Pisciotta	May 25 vs. Atlanta Mike Cather
12	May 31 vs. Boston Billy Muffett	May 1 vs. Chicago Cubs Rod Beck	May 27 vs. Philadelphia Darrin Winston
13	June 2 vs. Chicago White Sox Cal Mclish	May 8 vs. New York Mets Rick Reed	May 27 vs. Philadelphia Wayne Gomes
14	June 3 vs. Chicago White Sox Bob Shaw	May 12 vs. Milwaukee Paul Wagner	June 1 vs. Florida Ryan Dempster
15	June 4 vs. Chicago White Sox Russ Kemmerer	May 14 vs. Atlanta Kevin Millwood	June 1 vs. Florida Oscar Henriquez
16	June 6 vs. Minnesota Ed Palmquist	May 16 vs. Florida Livan Hernandez	June 3 vs. Florida Livan Hernandez
17	June 7 vs. Minnesota Pedro Ramos	May 18 vs. Florida Jesus Sanchez	June 5 vs. Chicago White Sox Jim Parque
18	June 9 vs. Kansas City Ray Herbert	May 19 vs. Philadelphia Tyler Green	June 6 vs. Chicago White Sox Carlos Castillo

BASEBALL STATS

NO.	MARIS	McGWIRE	SOSA
19	June 11 vs. Los Angeles Eli Grba	May 19 vs. Philadelphia Tyler Green	June 7 vs. Chicago White Sox James Baldwin
20	June 11 vs. Los Angeles Johnny James	May 19 vs. Philadelphia Wayne Gomes	June 8 vs. Minnesota LaTroy Hawkins
21	June 13 vs. Cleveland Jim Perry	May 22 vs. San Francisco Mark Gardner	June 13 vs. Philadelphia Mark Portugal
22	June 14 vs. Cleveland Gary Bell	May 23 vs. San Francisco Rich Rodriguez	June 15 vs. Milwaukee Cal Eldred
23	June 17 vs. Detroit Don Mossi	May 23 vs. San Francisco John Johnstone	June 15 vs. Milwaukee Cal Eldred
24	June 18 vs. Detroit Jerry Casale	May 24 vs. San Francisco Robb Nen	June 15 vs. Milwaukee Cal Eldred
25	June 19 vs. Kansas City Jim Archer	May 25 vs. Colorado John Thomson	June 17 vs. Milwaukee Bronswell Patrick
26	June 20 vs. Kansas City Joe Nuxhall	May 29 vs. San Diego Dan Miceli	June 19 vs. Philadelphia Carlton Loewer
27	June 22 vs. Kansas City Norm Bass	May 30 vs. San Diego Andy Ashby	June 19 vs. Philadelphia Carlton Loewer

NO.	MARIS	McGWIRE	SOSA
28	July 1 vs. Washington Dave Sisler	June 5 vs. San Francisco Orel Hershiser	June 20 vs. Philadelphia Matt Beech
29	July 2 vs. Washington Pete Burnside	June 8 vs. Chicago White Sox Jason Bere	June 20 vs. Philadelphia Toby Borland
30	July 2 vs. Washington Johnny Klippstein	June 10 vs. Chicago White Sox Jim Parque	June 21 vs. Philadelphia Tyler Green
31	July 4 vs. Detroit Frank Lary	June 12 vs. Arizona Andy Benes	June 24 vs. Detroit Seth Greisinger
32	July 5 vs. Cleveland Frank Funk	June 17 vs. Houston Jose Lima	June 25 vs. Detroit Brian Moehler
33	July 9 vs. Boston Bill Monbouquette	June 18 vs. Houston Shane Reynolds	June 30 vs. Arizona Alan Embree
34	July 13 vs. Chicago White Sox Early Wynn	June 24 vs. Cleveland Jaret Wright	July 9 vs. Milwaukee Jeff Juden
35	July 15 vs. Chicago White Sox Ray Herbert	June 25 vs. Cleveland Dave Burba	July 10 vs. Milwaukee Scott Karl
36	July 21 vs. Boston Bill Monbouquette	June 27 vs. Minnesota Mike Trombley	July 17 vs. Florida Kirt Ojala

BASEBALL STATS

NO.	MARIS	McGWIRE	SOSA
37	July 25 vs. Chicago White Sox Frank Baumann	June 30 vs. Kansas City Glendon Rusch	July 22 vs. Montreal Miguel Batista
38	July 25 vs. Chicago White Sox Don Larsen	July 11 vs. Houston Billy Wagner	July 26 vs. N.Y. Mets Rick Reed
39	July 25 vs. Chicago White Sox Russ Kemmerer	July 12 vs. Houston Sean Bergman	July 27 vs. Arizona Willie Blair
40	July 25 vs. Chicago White Sox Warren Hacker	July 12 vs. Houston Scott Elarton	July 27 vs. Arizona Alan Embree
41	August 4 vs. Minnesota Camilo Pascual	July 17 vs. Los Angeles Brian Bohanon	July 28 vs. Arizona Bob Wolcott
42	August 11 vs. Washington Pete Burnside	July 17 vs. Los Angeles Antonio Osuna	July 31 vs. Colorado Jamey Wright
43	August 12 vs. Washington Dick Donovan	July 20 vs. San Diego Brian Boehringer	August 5 vs. Arizona Andy Benes
44	August 13 vs. Washington Bernie Daniels	July 26 vs. Colorado John Thomson	August 8 vs. St. Louis Rich Croushere
45	August 13 vs. Washington Marty Kutyna	July 28 vs. Milwaukee Mike Myers	August 10 vs. San Francisco Russ Ortiz
46	August 15 vs. Chicago White Sox Juan Pizarro	August 8 vs. Chicago Cubs Mark Clark	August 10 vs. San Francisco Chris Brock

NO.	MARIS	McGWIRE	SOSA
47	August 16 vs. Chicago White Sox Billy Pierce	August 11 vs. New York Mets Bobby Jones	August 16 vs. Houston Sean Bergman
48	August 16 vs. Chicago White Sox Billy Pierce	August 19 vs. Chicago Cubs Matt Karchner	August 19 vs. St. Louis Kent Bottenfield
49	August 20 vs. Cleveland Jim Perry	August 19 vs. Chicago Cubs Terry Mulholland	August 21 vs. San Francisco Orel Herschiser
50	August 22 vs. Los Angeles Ken McBride	August 20 vs. New York Mets Willie Blair	August 23 vs. Houston Jose Lima
51	August 26 vs. Kansas City Jerry Walker	August 20 vs. New York Mets Rick Reed	August 23 vs. Houston Jose Lima
52	September 2 vs. Detroit Frank Lary	August 22 vs. Pittsburgh Francisco Cordova	August 26 vs. Cincinnati Brett Tomko
53	September 2 vs. Detroit Hank Aguirre	August 23 vs. Pittsburgh Ricardo Rincon	August 28 vs. Colorado John Thompson
54	September 6 vs. Washington Tom Cheney	August 26 vs. Florida Justin Speier	August 30 vs. Colorado Darryl Kile
55	September 7 vs. Cleveland Dick Stigman	August 30 vs. Atlanta Dennis Martinez	August 31 vs. Cincinnati Brett Tomko
56	September 9 vs. Cleveland Mudcat Grant	September 1 vs. Florida Livan Hernandez	September 2 vs. Cincinnati Jason Bere

BASEBALL STATS

NO.	MARIS	McGWIRE	SOSA
57	September 16 vs. Detroit Frank Lary	September 1 vs. Florida Donn Pall	September 4 vs. Pittsburgh Jason Schmidt
58	September 17 vs. Detroit Terry Fox	September 2 vs. Florida B. Edmondson	September 5 vs. Pittsburgh Sean Lawrence
59	September 20 vs. Baltimore Milt Pappas	September 2 vs. Florida Rob Standifer	September 11 vs. Milwaukee Bill Pulsipher
60	September 26 vs. Baltimore Jack Fisher	September 5 vs. Cincinnati Dennis Reyes	September 12 vs. Milwaukee Valerio de los Santos
61	October 1 vs. Boston Tracy Stallard	September 7 vs. Chicago Cubs Mike Morgan	September 13 vs. Milwaukee Bronswell Patrick
62		September 8 vs. Chicago Cubs Steve Trachsel	September 13 vs. Milwaukee Eric Plunk
63		September 15 vs. Pittsburgh Jason Christiansen	September 16 vs. San Diego Brian Boehringer
64		September 18 vs. Milwaukee Rafael Roque	September 23 vs. Milwaukee Rafael Roque
65		September 20 vs. Milwaukee Scott Karl	September 23 vs. Milwaukee Rod Henderson

**Through September 24, 1998*

POWERQUOTES

MAKE 'EM SAY "WOW!"

"It's two against one at the plate, the pitcher and catcher versus you. When I'm up there, I'm thinking. 'Try everything you want. Rub up the ball. Move the fielders around. Throw me hard stuff, soft stuff. Try anything. I'm still going to hit that ball.' I love to hit that little round [ball] out of the park and make 'em say 'Wow!'"

—Reggie Jackson

Ken Griffey Jr. has one of the sweetest swings in baseball. Only 28 years old, he already has 347 career home runs, and is considered to be the greatest threat to Hank Aaron's career home run total of 755.

KEN GRIFFEY JR.

NAME:	George (Ken) Kenneth Griffey Jr.
BIRTHDATE:	November 21, 1969
BIRTHPLACE:	Donora, Pennsylvania
HEIGHT:	6'3"
WEIGHT:	195
DRAFTED:	1st Round, June 1987
POSITION:	Center Field
UNIFORM NUMBER:	24
BATS:	Left
THROWS:	Left

CAREER HIGHLIGHTS

SEASONS PLAYED:	10
CURRENT TEAM:	Seattle Mariners, signed through 2000.
BATTING AVERAGE:	.302
HOME RUNS:	347
HITS:	1562
RBIs:	1009
ALL STAR GAMES:	6
ALL-STAR BATTING AVERAGE:	.444

KEN GRIFFEY JR.

THE "30-30" CLUB

One of baseball's great accomplishments is hitting 30 home runs and stealing 30 bases in the same season. Here are the men who did it, including Sosa—who has achieved this feat twice!

PLAYER	TEAM	YEAR	GAMES	HR	SB
Willie Mays	NY Giants	1956	152	36	40
Willie Mays	NY Giants	1957	152	35	38
Hank Aaron	Milwaukee	1963	161	44	31
Bobby Bonds	San Francisco	1969	158	32	45
Bobby Bonds	San Francisco	1973	160	39	43
Dale Murphy	Atlanta	1983	162	36	30
Eric Davis	Cincinnati	1987	129	37	50
Howard Johnson	NY Mets	1987	157	36	32

THE 30-30 CLUB

PLAYER	TEAM	YEAR	GAMES	HR	SB
Darryl Strawberry	NY Mets	1987	154	39	36
Jose Canseco	A's	1988	158	42	40
Howard Johnson	NY Mets	1989	153	36	41
Ron Gant	Atlanta	1990	152	32	33
Barry Bonds	Pittsburgh	1990	151	33	52
Ron Gant	Atlanta	1991	154	32	34
Howard Johnson	NY Mets	1991	156	38	30
Barry Bonds	Pittsburgh	1992	140	34	39
Sammy Sosa	**Chicago**	**1993**	**159**	**33**	**36**

PLAYER	TEAM	YEAR	GAMES	HR	SB
Barry Bonds	San Francisco	1995	144	33	31
Sammy Sosa	**Chicago**	**1995**	**144**	**36**	**34**
Barry Bonds	San Francisco	1996	158	42	40
Ellis Burks	Colorado	1996	156	40	32
Dante Bichette	Colorado	1996	159	31	31
Larry Walker	Colorado	1997	153	49	33
Barry Bonds	San Francisco	1997	159	40	37
Raul Mondesi	Los Angeles	1997	159	30	32
Jeff Bagwell	Houston	1997	162	43	31

WHERE I COME FROM

"I'll never forget where I come from. These are my people. I'm proud of the United States. They've given me everything I have. But I have to remember these are my people, people I have to take care of, people I have to give jobs to. This is my life."

—Sammy Sosa

(Speaking of his hometown of San Pedro de Macoris)

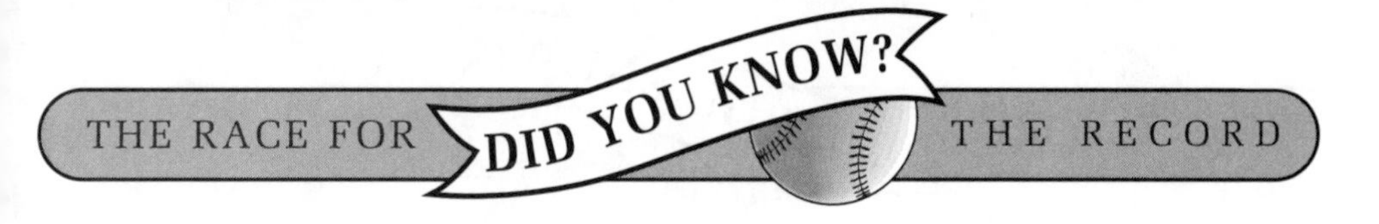

"PAPA"

Sosa's first baseball glove was a cut off milk carton—it's all he could afford.

Bill Chase, who came to the Dominican Republic from the Northeastern United States in 1979 to purchase a factory, saw Sosa playing baseball with other boys.

He recognized a natural ability and bought Sammy his first real glove.

To this day, Sosa calls Chase, "Papa."

IT'S IN THE CARDS

Sosa and McGwire's home run race has sent prices for their sports memorabilia sky rocketing.

A Mark McGwire rookie card from Topps would have gone for $25 to $30 at the most in 1997. Recently, one was picked up for $585 at an e-mail auction.

Sosa's not doing badly either! A mint condition rookie card that cost $120 in August of 1998, was selling for $480 just one month later.

Seasons With Two or More Players Hitting 50 Homers

*1998—Mark McGwire (65), Sammy Sosa (65), and Ken Griffey Jr. (55)

1997 — Mark McGwire (58) and Ken Griffey Jr. (56)

1996 — Mark McGwire (52) and Brady Anderson (50)

1961 — Roger Maris (61) and Mickey Mantle (54)

1947 — Ralph Kiner (51) and Johnny Mize (51)

** Through September 24, 1998*

SOSA'S JULY FIREWORKS

Sosa edged McGwire for the month, 9-to-8, just average numbers for the two big guns. The race was getting interesting, with more explosives ahead in August.

AB	—	107	**RBI**	—	29
G	—	27	**BB**	—	12
H	—	28	**SLG**	—	.561
HR	—	9	**AVG**	—	.262

A MAJOR LEAGUE BARGAIN!

In 1998 Sosa takes home a cool $5.5 million, with $2.5 million deferred. In 1999, he will receive $9 million; $11 million in 2000; and $12 million in 2001. Not bad for a shoeshine boy from the Dominican Republic. And if he continues to perform anywhere close to his 1998 standards, by the year 2002, as Sosa is celebrating his 33rd birthday, Cubs president Andy MacPhail's $40 million investment will look like the best deal in baseball.

MacPhail says he took a chance on Sosa on the basis of his talent and determination. "At the same time, I looked at Sammy as an investment in character and talent, I saw a guy getting better." And get better he did! His explosive home run pace has already made him a baseball bargain!

AMAZING YEARS IN BASEBALL
1998

- 1998 is truly amazing because two men have accomplished in one year, what only two other men did in the entire history of baseball: hit more than 60 home runs in one season.
- Ken Griffey Jr. has hit more than 50 homers.
- Barry Bonds became the first player in Major League history to accumulate 400 homers and 400 stolen bases in a career.
- Cal Ripken Jr.'s streak of consecutive games played came to an end at 2,632.

AMAZING YEARS IN BASEBALL
1930

- Cubs' player Hack Wilson hit 56 homers and had 190 RBIs, still a Major League record.
- Bill Terry was the last National Leaguer to hit over .400, with a .401 average.
- The batting average for the entire National League was .303!

AMAZING YEARS IN BASEBALL
1941

- Ted Williams hit .406, the last Major Leaguer to do so.
- Joe DiMaggio hit in 56 straight games—which is still the Major League record.
- America mourns the death of Lou Gehrig from amyotrophic lateral sclerosis, which would become commonly known as "Lou Gehrig's Disease".
- The St. Louis Cardinals edge the Brooklyn Dodgers for the National League pennant. The teams won 106 and 104 games respectively.

AMAZING YEARS IN BASEBALL
1968

- 1968 was the year of pitchers: the Major League batting average was the lowest ever at .237, with only 6.84 runs per game (lowest since 1908).
- Denny McLain of the Tigers was the first pitcher since Dizzy Dean in 1934 to win 30 or more games (31-6).
- Don Drysdale of the Dodgers pitched 58 consecutive scoreless innings.
- Bob Gibson of the Cardinals set the National League record with a 1.12 earned run average.

JUST DOING HIS JOB

"He's one of those guys who just goes out and does his job. He's in the lineup every day and if the pitchers are giving him good balls to hit, he will hit them out of the ballpark. He doesn't really think about it that much. He just goes about his business and he has some fun with it, too."

—Billy Williams

(Cubs dugout coach and Hall of Famer.)

The crowd at Wrigley roars in approval as Sosa rounds the bases after hitting number 61!

PLAZA 30-30

Sosa built a monument celebrating his 1993 season—his first year to hit 30 homers and steal 30 bases—and dedicated it to the shoe shine boys of his hometown, San Pedro de Macoris.

Within Plaza 30-30, the only shopping center of its kind in the Dominican Republic, you will find businesses that Sosa has set up for his brothers and sisters—a boutique, hair salon, and "Club Sammy" to name a few.

DID YOU KNOW?

In the middle of Plaza 30-30 is a statue of Sosa in his Cubs uniform and a wishing well titled, Fountain of the Shoeshine Boys. All coins thrown into the fountain are donated to charity.

GEORGE HERMAN "BABE" RUTH

THE RUTH LEGACY

- Babe Ruth began his career as a left-handed pitcher for the Boston Red Sox in 1914. He compiled a 78-40 record in four years with the Red Sox.
- Ruth became a full time outfielder in 1919, setting a new home run record of 29 and leading the league in runs, RBI's, and slugging percentage.
- He led the league in home runs eight of the next ten years.
- Ruth was the first man to hit 20, 30, 40, 50, and 60 home runs in a single season.

THE RUTH LEGACY

- Ruth led the league in home runs 12 times, runs 8 times, RBIs 6 times, and slugging percentage 13 times during his twenty full seasons.
- Ruth's lifetime batting average was .342.
- He was the all time leader in home run percentages (11.8) until Mark McGwire caught him in 1998. Walks (20560). Slugging percentage (.690).
- Ruth was one of the first five elected to the Hall of Fame in 1936, receiving 95% of the votes possible (215 out of 226).
- Ruth was one of only two people (Reggie Jackson being the other) to ever hit three home runs in a World Series game and is the only one to do it twice (1926 & 1928).

GEORGE HERMAN "BABE" RUTH

THE RUTH LEGACY

- Ruth was so well known internationally that during World War II, when Japanese soldiers wanted to taunt Americans across the battle lines, they would shout: "To hell with Babe Ruth!"
- Ruth is credited with the invention of the modern baseball bat. He was the first player to order a bat with a knob on the end of the handle. Louisville Slugger produced the bat with which he hit 29 home runs in 1919.
- Ruth holds the record for the longest complete game victory in World Series history. In 1916, as a member of the Boston Red Sox, Ruth went 14 innings to defeat the New York Giants 2-1.

GEORGE HERMAN "BABE" RUTH

THE FICKLE WINDS OF TRADE

Sosa began his career in 1985 as a non-drafted free agent for Texas. In 1989, he was traded to the Chicago White Sox with pitcher Wilson Alvarez and infielder Scott Fletcher for outfielder Harold Baines and infielder Fred Manrique. In 1992, he was traded to the Chicago Cubs with pitcher Ken Patterson for outfielder George Bell, a fellow Dominican.

When Sosa came to the Cubs in a "two for the price of one" deal for Bell (a proven slugger and the 1987 American League MVP), the Sox obviously speculated that they had made a good trade. But Bell's sizzling career in Toronto, which included 47 home runs in 1987, had already begun to cool off during his brief stint with the Cubs. Bell's career ended in 1993 with only 13 homers during that season.

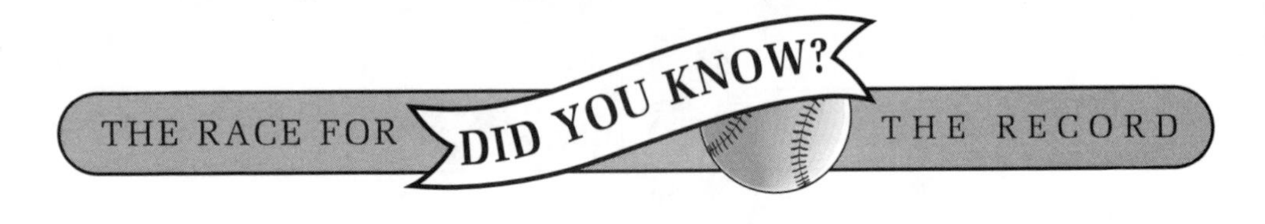

SAMMY CLAUS

In addition to the contributions Sammy Sosa has made to the medical, educational, and economic needs of his native Dominican Republic, he has also earned a reputation for making a difference here in the States.

Sosa won his way into the hearts of young Chicago fans by providing game tickets on "Sammy Sundays" for children who would not otherwise be able to attend.

In December of 1997, Sosa provided more than 7,000 children with toys and gifts through his first annual "Sammy Claus World Tour". His generosity not only touched the lives of children in his hometown of San Pedro de Marcoris, but also brightened the Christmas season for families in Santo Domingo, Washington D.C., Philadelphia, New York, Chicago, and Miami.

#59: A DRIVE ON SHEFFIELD AVE.

On September 11 Sosa went on a home run binge to catch McGwire at 62, starting with a fifth inning smash onto Sheffield Avenue against Bill Pulsipher of the Milwaukee Brewers.

It ended a drought of 21 At-Bats without a home run, making Sosa only the fourth man in history to reach 59 home runs.

The 464-foot shot was his second longest of the year.

SAMMY'S AUGUST HEAT

Sosa entered August with 42 homers, three behind McGwire. But both men finished the month at 55—this race would go down to the wire!

AB	—	115	**RBI**	—	28
G	—	28	**BB**	—	16
H	—	37	**SLG**	—	.678
HR	—	13	**AVG**	—	.322

The Maris Line

NAME AT BIRTH:	Roger Eugene Maras*
BIRTHPLACE:	Hibbing, Minnesota
RAISED:	Fargo, North Dakota
VITAL STATS:	6', 204 pounds
DIED:	December 14, 1985, in Houston, Texas
POSITION:	Right Field
BATTED:	Left
TEAMS:	Cleveland Indians, Kansas City Athletics, New York Yankees, St. Louis Cardinals
AWARDS:	American League MVP in 1960 and 1961

CAREER NUMBERS: 1,465 games

5,101 At-Bats

1,325 hits

275 home runs

851 runs batted in

.260 batting average

* When asked why he changed the spelling of his name, Maris answered, "It's immaterial."

FANS BOYCOTT MARIS

The New York Yankees, an exciting team on its way to a World Series showdown with the Cincinnati Reds, had clinched the American League pennant in a tough playoff race in 1961. You would expect huge crowds as Maris approached Ruth's record.

But because New York never warmed to Maris, the 1960 American League MVP, and because many were not excited about him breaking what was considered to be an unbreakable record, a mere 23,000 spectators showed up on October 1, 1961, to see his historic blast.

NO JEALOUSY

"He deserves it because he has been putting up some big numbers the last three or four years. I don't have time for jealousy or anything like that. I'm happy for him. I hope he continues doing it. For me, he's the man. If he's the MVP, that's fine. I have a lot of years left."

—Sammy Sosa

(Commenting on attention given to Mark McGwire.)

THE MINOR LEAGUES

Year	Club	Avg.	Games	At-Bats	Runs	Hits	Doubles
1986	Gulf Coast-R	275	61	229	38	63	19
1987	Gastonia-A	.279	129	519	73	145	27
1988	Charlotte, FL-A	.229	131	507	70	116	13
1989	Tulsa-AA	.297	66	273	45	81	15
1989	Ok. City-AAA	.103	10	39	2	4	2
1989	Vancouver-AAA	.367	13	49	7	18	3
1991	Vancouver-AAA	.267	32	116	19	31	7
1992	Iowa-AAA	.316	5	19	3	6	2

THE MINOR LEAGUES

Triples	Homers	RBI	BB	SO	Stolen Bases
1	4	28	22	51	11
4	11	59	21	123	22
12	9	51	35	106	42
4	7	31	15	52	16
0	0	3	2	8	4
0	1	5	7	6	3
2	3	19	17	32	9
0	0	1	1	2	5

KISS IT GOODBYE

FAVORITE PHRASES BY ANNOUNCERS WHEN A HOME RUN IS HIT:

"Holy Cow! That ball's out of here!"
—Harry Caray

"Bye-bye baby."
—Russ Hodges

"Forget it."
—Vin Scully

"Goodbye, baseball!"
—Dick Risenhoover

"Goodbye, Dolly Grey."
—Leo Durocher

DID YOU KNOW?

"Open the window, Aunt Minnie, here it comes."
—Rosey Roswell

"Tell it goodbye!"
—Jon Miller

"That ball is history."
—Eric Nagel

"They usually show movies on a flight like that."
—Ken Coleman

"Whoo, boy! Next time around, bring me back my stomach."
—Jack Brickhouse

SOSA'S SEPTEMBER RAMPAGE

McGwire hit number 65 on September 20, and gave a sigh of relief. But Sosa wouldn't let him relax for long. Three days later, Sosa hit two homers to even the race again!

AB	—	86	**RBI**	—	20
G	—	21	**BB**	—	12
H	—	22	**SLG**	—	.616
HR	—	10	**AVG**	—	.256

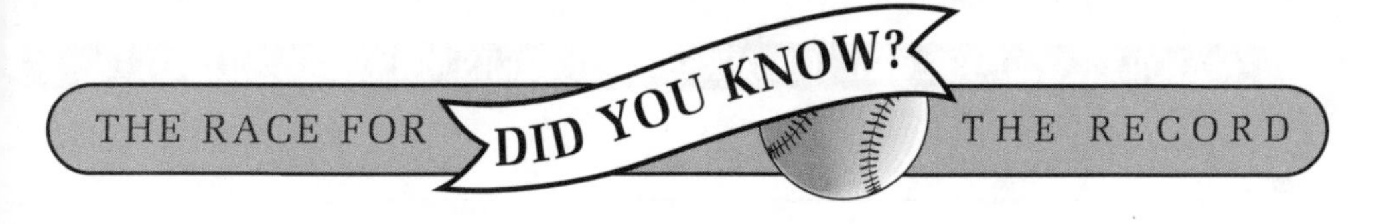

JAPAN'S "SULTAN OF SWAT"

Sadaharu Oh of the Tokyo Giants, still holds the record for the most home runs in a career, with 868. From 1965-1973, Oh led the Giants to victory in nine straight Japan Series. Oh played only 130 games a year, and was walked so often, that he often came to the plate fewer than 300 times. Most Major League Baseball home run champs have historically had more than 500 At-Bats.

MAJOR LEAGUE RECORD HOLDERS FOR HOMERS MONTH-BY-MONTH

PLAYER	TEAM	YEAR
MARCH: 1 Home Run		
Darren Bragg	Seattle	1996
Frank Thomas	Chicago White Sox	1996
Mark McGwire	St. Louis	1998
APRIL: 13 Home Runs		
Ken Griffey Jr.	Seattle	1997
MAY: 16 Home Runs		
Mickey Mantle	NY Yankees	1956

MAJOR LEAGUE RECORD HOLDERS FOR HOMERS MONTH-BY-MONTH

PLAYER	TEAM	YEAR
JUNE: 20 Home Runs		
Sammy Sosa	Chicago Cubs	1998
JULY: 15 Home Runs		
Joe DiMaggio	NY Yankees	1937
Hank Greenberg	Detroit	1938
Joe Adcock	Milwaukee	1956
Juan Gonzalez	Texas	1996
Albert Belle	Chicago White Sox	1998
AUGUST: 18 Home Runs		
Rudy York	NY Yankees	1937

MAJOR LEAGUE RECORD HOLDERS FOR HOMERS MONTH-BY-MONTH

PLAYER	TEAM	YEAR
SEPTEMBER: 17 Home Runs		
Babe Ruth	NY Yankees	1927
Albert Belle	Cleveland	1995
OCTOBER: 4 Home Runs		
Ned Williamson	Chicago Cubs	1884
Gus Zernial	Chicago White Sox	1950
Mike Schmidt	Philadelphia	1980
George Brett	Kansas City	1985
Ron Kittle	Chicago White Sox	1985
Dave Parker	Cincinnati	1985
Wally Joyner	California	1987

400 TOTAL BASES

In 1998, Sosa joined 23 other players who have collected 400 total bases in a single season.

The list reads like the Who's-Who of Major League Baseball.

(Note on Total Bases: A single is worth one base; a double two-bases; a triple three bases; and a homer four bases.)

400 TOTAL BASES

PLAYER	TEAM	YEAR	BASES
Babe Ruth	NY Yankees	1921	457
Rogers Hornsby	Cardinals	1922	450
Lou Gehrig	NY Yankees	1927	447
Chuck Klein	Phillies	1930	445
Jimmie Foxx	Athletics	1932	438
Stan Musial	Cardinals	1948	429
Hack Wilson	Chicago Cubs	1930	423
Chuck Klein	Phillies	1932	420
Lou Gehrig	NY Yankees	1930	419
Joe DiMaggio	NY Yankees	1937	418
Babe Ruth	NY Yankees	1927	417
Babe Ruth	Dodgers	1930	416

400 TOTAL BASES

PLAYER	TEAM	YEAR	BASES
Lou Gehrig	NY Yankees	1931	410
Larry Walker	Rockies	1997	409
Lou Gehrig	NY Yankees	1929	409
Rogers Hornsby	Chicago Cubs	1929	409
Sammy Sosa	**Chicago Cubs**	**1998**	**406***
Jim Rice	Red Sox	1978	406
Joe Medwick	Cardinals	1937	406
Hal Trosky	Indians	1936	405
Chuck Klein	Phillies	1929	405
Lou Gehrig	NY Yankees	1936	403
Jimmie Foxx	Athletics	1933	403
Henry "Hank" Aaron	Braves	1959	400

*Through September 24, 1998

TRUE OR FALSE?

- The Major League Baseball Hall of Fame is in Canton, Ohio.
- The game of baseball was invented by Thomas Edison.
- Abner Doubleday, a Civil War General, was the first commissioner of baseball.

(Turn to page 138 for the answers.)

McGwire takes a mighty swing as he tries to hold off Sosa in the home run race.

ANSWERS TO TRUE/FALSE QUESTIONS:

- **False**. Baseball's Hall of Fame is actually in Cooperstown, New York, where baseball was alledged to have started.
- **False**. Edison invented the light bulb—not baseball!
- **Maybe**. Abner Doubleday was a Civil War General—and the man credited with founding baseball. However, he claimed no connection to the sport.

The Pitch

Here's a few pitchers who will be remembered forever for home run pitches they served up:

Eric Plunk:	**Sammy Sosa's 62nd homer in a season**
Tom Zachary:	Babe Ruth's 60th
Tracy Stallard:	Roger Maris' 61st
Al Downing:	Hank Aaron's 715th
Eric Show:	Pete Rose's 4,123rd hit
Steve Trachsel:	Mark McGwire's 62nd
Ralph Branca:	Bobby Richardson's "shot heard 'round the world"

#60 RARE AIR

Sosa joined the exclusive 60-Homer Club on September 12, 1998, with a three run, seventh inning blast off Valerio de los Santos of the Milwaukee Brewers.

The Cubs were trailing 12-5 at the time, and Sosa's four-bagger sparked the Cubs to a 15-12 win as they continued to fight for the final National League playoff spot.

THE RACE FOR DID YOU KNOW? THE RECORD

The homer was Sosa's 33rd in Wrigley Field in 1998, tying Hack Wilson's 1930 Club record.

The 430-foot slam sailed over the left field bleachers and landed on Waveland Avenue. Herb Neurauter caught the ball and returned it to Sosa in exchange for an autographed baseball.

This brought Sosa to within two homers of McGwire—a gap he closed with two homers in his next game.

1998 HOME RUN PARADE

In the 78 years since Babe Ruth hit 54 home runs in 1920 (to become the first to break the 40 homer barrier) only 103 men have hit 43 or more homers in a single season.

In 1998, at least 11 men equaled or bested that mark by September 24—

THE RACE FOR DID YOU KNOW? THE RECORD

PLAYER	TEAM	HR
Mark McGwire	St. Louis Cardinals	65*
Sammy Sosa	**Chicago Cubs**	**65***
Ken Griffey Jr.	Seattle Mariners	55
Greg Vaughn	San Diego Padres	49
Albert Belle	Chicago White Sox	47
Jose Canseco	Toronto Blue Jays	46
Vinny Castilla	Colorado Rockies	45
Juan Gonzalez	Texas Rangers	45
Manny Ramirez	Cleveland Indians	45
Rafael Palmeiro	Baltimore Orioles	43
Andres Galarraga	Atlanta Braves	43

**Through September 24, 1998*

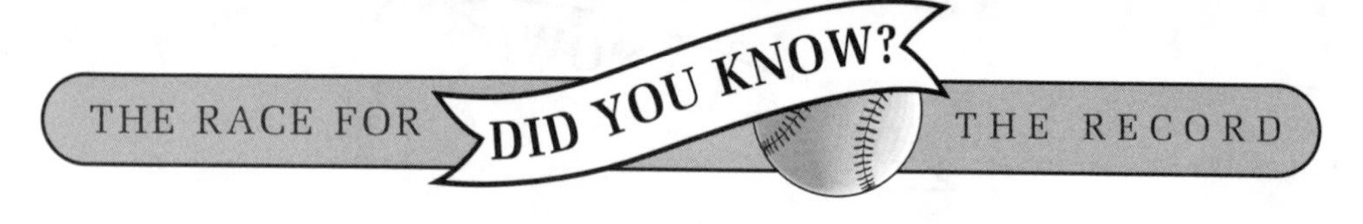

THE BIG HACK ATTACK

McGwire and Sosa caught and surpassed the Cubs' Hack Wilson's National League record of 56 home runs in 1930—a record that stood for 68 years. Wilson's Major League record of 190 runs batted in, appears to be safe for another year. The only serious challenges to that amazing mark were mounted by Lou Gehrig with 184 in 1931, and Hank Greenberg with 183 in 1937. Sosa has 154 runs batted in so far in 1998.

Some baseball historians note that Wilson's record came during the year of the "live ball". The batting average of all players in the National League that year (1930) was .303. Six of the eight teams batted higher than .300. Philadelphia hit .319 as a team, a record that will probably never be broken. Seventy-one players hit .300 or better that year!

FOR MOTHER ONLY

Sosa has already sent home run ball number 61 to the Hall of Fame, and has promised number 62 to Cooperstown if he ever gets it back.

But he says "no way" on number 63. Why?

He will present that one to his mother.

DID YOU KNOW?

THE HOPE OF A NATION

Sammy Sosa's success has made him a legend in his native Dominican Republic and stoked the flames of an immense national pride. It seems that the shoeshine boy from San Pedro de Marcoris has become a beacon of hope for a nation that is only now emerging from centuries of poverty and oppression.

Each time Sammy Sosa comes to bat, a nation holds its collective breath and millions of Dominicans watch with anticipation as their favorite native son takes a swing. His achievements grace the front pages of Dominican newspapers and serve as the main topic of discussion on Dominican TV. Sammy's quest has become their own.

Sosa slams number 62 to catch McGwire in breaking Roger Maris' record for home runs in a season.

#'s 61 AND 62!
GOODBYE BABE AND ROGER—HELLO MARK!

Sosa passed Ruth and Maris—and caught McGwire with two blasts on September 13, 1998, as Chicago won a wild ten inning game over Milwaukee to keep a one-game lead over the Mets in the wildcard race.

Home run number 61 was a two run round tripper in the fifth inning off Bronswell Patrick. Sosa's second shot, a 480-footer off Eric Plunk, came in the bottom of the ninth with the Cubs trailing 8-10.

FOR THE HISTORY BOOKS

DID YOU KNOW?

Sosa was on deck in the tenth inning with a chance to hit number 63—and tie the score—when teammate Mark Grace ended the game with a solo home run.

Sosa's teammates carried him off the field to celebrate the win. This was Sosa's tenth multiple home run game of the year.

GREAT SEPTEMBER HOME RUN RACES

1927

Ruth entered September with a 43-41 lead over teammate Gehrig. Then on September 6, Gehrig briefly took the lead with his 45th homer of the season, but Ruth followed with three home runs in that same game, and two more the next game for a total of 49. He hit 11 more in his last 20 games to finish with 60, while Gehrig finished the year with 49.

1961

Maris and Mantle were neck-and-neck at the beginning of September, with Maris holding a 56-53 lead. However, Mantle developed a hip abscess after receiving a flu shot and missed 18 games. Mantle finished the season with 54 homers, while Maris set the new Major League record with 61.

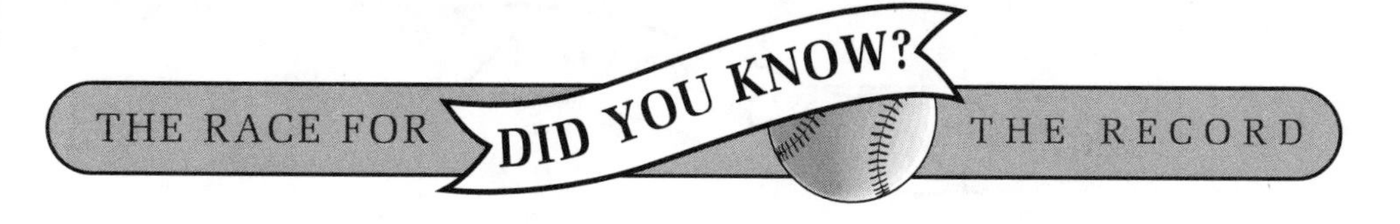

1998

Sosa didn't catch Griffey until July 28 when he hit number 41. But McGwire was busy hitting number 45 that same day. McGwire and Sosa began the month of September tied at 55 homers each. McGwire hit four homers in the first two days of the month and beat Sosa to 60 by one week, and then to 62 by five days. But Sosa caught McGwire at 62 on September 13th and then at 63 on September 16th. McGwire pulled away with 64 and 65, that is, until September 23rd when Sammy blasted two out of the park against the Milwaukee Brewers.

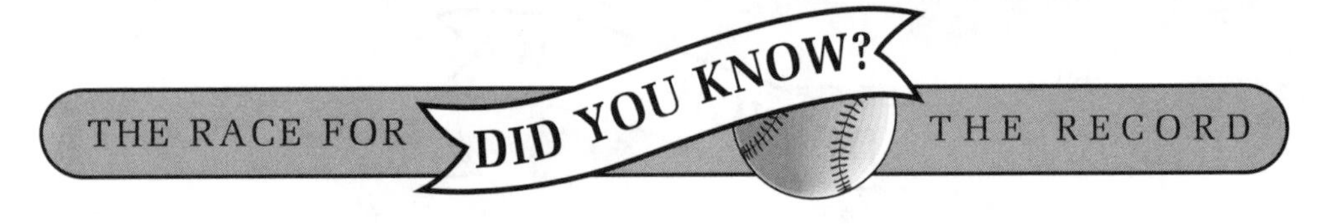

THE REAL FIGHT FOR 62?

"Moe" Mullins claims he came up with Sosa's home run ball number 62 on Waveland Avenue, outside the left field fence at Wrigley Field.

But then he claims 50 people jumped on him, with one man biting his left hand and wresting the ball from him. Moe plans to file a police report.

The person who nabbed the ball, Brandan Cunningham, was taken into police custody for his own protection. A Chicago judge will decide what will be done with number 62.

Sosa's response? He laughed!

#63—A GRAND SLAM!

Sosa caught McGwire with 63 home runs on September 16 with a tiebreaking grand slam home run in the eighth inning, off San Diego Padres' pitcher, Brian Boehringer.

Sosa drove in all of the Cubs' runs in a 6-3 win to keep his team a half game ahead of the New York Mets in the race for the National League's final playoff spot.

Despite the home team's loss, the 49,891 spectators in San Diego gave Sosa a long standing ovation.

His left-field blast traveled 434 feet into the second deck of Jack Murphy stadium. Only 22 homers have traveled that far in the park's history.

Not only that, but Sosa tied his career best of 6 RBIs in a single game, and took the Major League lead with 154.

BASEBALL STATS

THE MAJOR LEAGUES

Year	Club	Avg.	Games	At-Bats	Runs	Hits	Doubles
1989	Texas	.238	25	84	8	20	3
1989	Chicago White Sox	.273	33	99	19	27	5
1990	Chicago White Sox	.233	153	532	72	124	26
1991	Chicago White Sox	.203	116	316	39	64	10
1992	Chicago Cubs	.260	67	262	41	68	7
1993	Chicago Cubs.	261	159	598	92	156	25
1994	Chicago Cubs	.300	105	426	59	128	17
1995	Chicago Cubs	.268	144	564	89	151	17
1996	Chicago Cubs	.273	124	498	84	136	21
1997	Chicago Cubs	.251	162	642	90	161	31
1998*	Chicago Cubs	.305	155	626	130	191	20

**Through September 24, 1998*

THE MAJOR LEAGUES

Triples	Homers	RBI	BB	SO	Stolen Bases
0	1	3	0	20	0
0	3	10	11	27	7
10	15	70	33	150	32
1	10	33	14	98	13
2	8	25	19	63	15
5	33	93	38	135	36
6	25	70	25	92	22
3	36	119	58	134	34
2	40	100	34	134	18
4	36	119	45	174	22
0	65	156	73	167	17

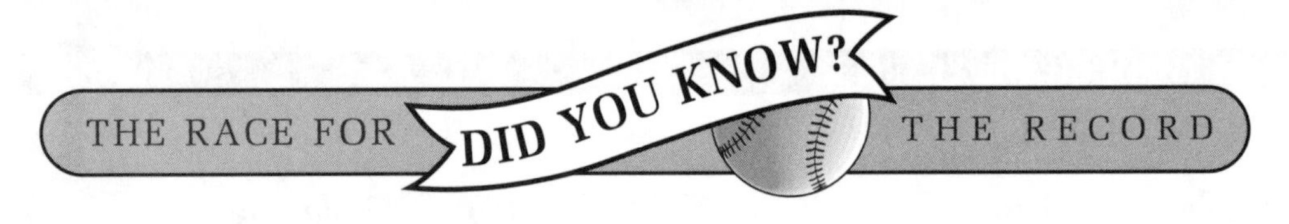

#'s 64 AND 65!
THE THRILL—AND THE AGONY

The thrill? Sosa tied the Major League record for multiple home run games in a single season, matching Hank Greenberg's 1938 record of 11, as he hit home runs 64 and 65 on September 23, 1998, against Milwaukee Brewers' pitchers Rafael Roque and Rod Henderson.

The agony? A costly error in the bottom of the ninth by Cubs' outfielder, Brant Brown, allowed the Brewers to score three runs for an 8-7 come-from-behind win. The Cubs remained in a tie with the NY Mets for the last National League playoff spot.

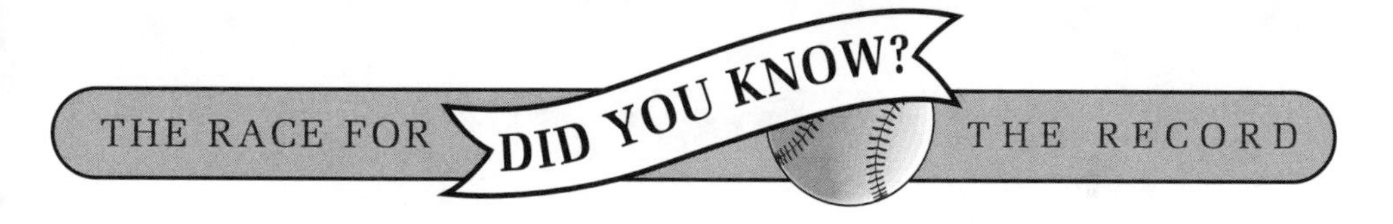

Sosa increased his RBI total for the year to 156, which is the fourth highest total in National League history.

Sosa was in a 0-for-21 batting slump entering the game. He walked in his first two plate appearances, then hit a 344-foot shot in the fifth inning, and a 410-foot slam in the sixth, once again pulling even with Mark McGwire for a league-leading 65 home runs.

POWERQUOTES

YOU NEVER KNOW!

"Why not 70?
You never know what can happen
in this game."

—Sammy Sosa

(When asked if he could surpass Roger Maris' mark of 61 home runs.)

#66 SAMMY AND MAC RACE TO 66

The home run duel between Sosa and McGwire hit epic proportions on Friday night, September 25! Sosa siezed the home run lead from McGwire with a 452-foot rocket off Jose Lima of the Astros. It was only the second time in the 1998 campaign that Sosa held the lead. But just 45 minutes later, McGwire answered with a missle off Shayne Bennett of the Expos to keep the race in a dead heat.

Despite Sosa's homer, his Cubs fell to the Astros 6-2, which put them in a three-way tie with the Mets and Giants for the final play off spot. With two games left in the season, that left two races to be decided--the NL wildcard spot and the home run title!

THE SAMMY SOSA FOUNDATION

A portion of all proceeds from this book
will be donated to The Sammy Sosa Foundation.

The Publisher encourages all readers to contribute to
this charity by sending a check to:

The Sammy Sosa Foundation
4917 NW 110th Terrace
Coral Springs, Florida 33076